Ink Your Name on Human Creativity

_____, aArts Champion
                Print Name

_____, aArts Champion
                Signature

_____
                Date

Big Bang Blossoming

Every human being has been touched by art, enriched by art, awakened and invigorated and inspired by art. Everyone has a poem or a story or a play or a dance or a painting or a song that enriched and reframed their lives. So I know everyone will eventually, if not immediately, align with igniting this new consciousness of the prerequisite, foundational, essential, and transcendent elements of art. And when they align with and understand this new comprehension of art, they will become an Everyone Creative Champion and support this Big Bang Blossoming of the arts.

Other Books by Patrick Muller

Healthcare Communication: A Rhetorical Handbook
I can cure your cancer with this poem

Forthcoming

My Oeuvre for $4 Billion
Art Genome: Mapping the 47 Dimensions and the Polyvalence
of a Work-of-Art

Nikos Sakethevan Publishing

Hills, Iowa ❖ Olomouc, Czechia

A
Modest Proposal
of
Immense Proportions

Patrick Muller

ISBN 978-1-257-89145-0

A
Modest Proposal
of
Immense Proportions

A Modest Proposal

A modest proposal of immense proportions, powered by you -- creative champion and profound storyteller -- powered by us, to nourish engaged and aware community, informed and civil dialogue, vibrant *a*Artsphere (*a*Arts ecosphere) personal enrichment and exuberance, and human actualization by igniting and sustaining a cultural substrate (specifically the Prairie Filaments Cultural Substrate) with eventually 728 invigoration modes, fueled by participarts in the Wowsa Club and fortified by satellite Red Door Neighborhood Catalysts and Cosmic Third Places to author conversational, collaborative, resilient, empathic, optimistic, adaptive, sentient, welcoming, curious, explorative, anchoring, critically thinking, and meaning making interactions in a complementary United *a*Arts of America.

A Modest Proposal of Immense Proportions

In November, 2020, 158,590,503 Americans voted across the political president to select the president who would lead the nation from 2021 - 2024.

I make this modest proposal: 158 million, or more, Americans earn their first badge ("I'm inking my name upon human creativity") in the Wowsa Club by expressing they are champions of their own creative human essence and of robust artistic conversations in their neighborhoods and communities that enrich all of humanity with this creativity. This modest proposal, followed through, will lead to an outcome of immense proportions: a sustainable, countrywide nutritive tapestry, infrastructure, or substrate that vibrantly supports the arts (and all the perspective, insight, understanding, and meaning they provide) and the enriching power of all our imaginations.

* In the 2020 Presidential Election, 81,286,358 people voted for Democrat Joe Biden; 74,255,839 for Republican Donald Trump;

1,865,616 for Libertarian Jo Jorgensen; 406,687 for Green Howie Hawkins; and 806,003 for assorted Other. This is a total of 158,590,503.

The Inaugural Wowsa Club Badge
I am inking my name on human creativity

Every human has an imagination and creative capacity.
Our stories and inquiries in letters, poems, novels, dances,
songs, symphonies, plays, spoken words, costumes,
fashions, rituals, festivals, cuisines, discussions, and other
forms give coalescing and enriched perspective, insight,
meaning, and understanding to our lives and world. I will
learn about by creativity, celebrate it, and cultivate it.

Wowsa Club Badges

The Wowsa Club is a fun mechanism for arts champions to chronicle and celebrate their support for the arts. For each badge earned, the badge earner will support the Prairie Filaments Cultural Substrate, a vibrant infrastructure that supports the arts at a foundational level. The badge earner will also support four different artists who will sign off on the badge*. The badge earners will also be able, if they so choose, to collect their badges in a handsome digital and/or physical album.*

The badges are nominal in price to give everyone access and to not pull down anyone's budget.

*These elements of the badges are in development and will be available in a year or two.

The United *a*Arts of America Flag

Dear Reader, of course you have noticed the graphic heading each one of these vignettes. It is the flag of our United *a*Arts of America. (More on *a*Art in a bit.) It can represent works-of-art on a wall -- either the paintings you own or a painter's exhibition. It can represent books in your library or an author's oeuvre. It can represent poems or journal entries you have reading. They can be albums/CDs you have acquired or a musician's oeuvre. They can be dates of plays, dances, films, or other performances on a cultural presenter's calendar. They can be a playwright or choreographer's ouevre.

I dislike that they are so orderly, linear, and static as we know life's orderliness is adaptability and revision; life's linearity is a wonderous wander; and life's static state is fluidity and dynamism. We do achieve pockets of order, delineation, and stasis -- represented with clarity and emphasis by the flag. The hollow square, however, reminds us we will soon break into a new version, ramble, and movement as we author our next moments of clarity and stability.

The empty square also represents imperfection and incompleteness -- both great attributes rather than deficiencies.

Mostly, however, the empty square represents two things. Firstly, it encourages you to always be open to newness and change and revision and growth. Secondly, it encourages to take that needed step, to connect with self-care, others, community, and the world -- even as one may feel overwhelmed. It encourages you to make that little contribution to our brilliance. And specifically it encourages you to make a nominal contribution (earn a Wowsa Club badge or two) to the unprecedented blossoming of the arts as we recognize they are prerequisite to humanity and our own actualization.

Art

I say this is a new consciousness and new comprehension of art; a Big Bang Blossoming of Art. But it's not. This is not an initiative about art; it's an initiative about *a*Art.

Art is the carburetor or even car that gets one on the summer road trip to the Grand Canyon. *a*Art is the road trip to the Grand Canyon. A profound difference, and think about that for as long as you need to for it to sink in.

I would say art is for quarters and *a*Art is for wholes. But you would have to understand much more about your actualizing humanity in meta-analytical ethnospheric understanding and you would have to inhabit much more of your actualizing humanity for it to ever be a constructive and understandable conversation for you. So we won't spend time on that discussion. The good news is *a*Art is accessible, and *a*Art will shepherd you towards that actualizing humanity.

Art is technique. *a*Art is perception. Art is the resolution of tension. *a*Art has already solved tension and engages more complex dialogues. Art is proclivitous beauty, mostly safe and tame truths, social marking, commodification, trophy taking, and something to. *a*Art is all of those things but only in ephemeral fractions.

*a*Art is so much more.

*a*Art

    *a*Art* is the ongoing dialogues, interactions, perceptions, interpretations, storytellings, meaning-makings, and learnings among artist, work-of-art, art presenters, and art enthusiasts. *a*Art is not a work-of-art. *a*Art is a work-of-art as organism living and metabolizing and understanding among all these dialogues, interactions, and milieus in which it finds itself.

    *a*Art is never static nor singular nor rigidly delineated. It is fluid, sentient, and conversational. This is reason an italicized lower case a precedes a perhaps

    *When people speak of art, they often mean fine art or visual art (painting, sculpture, metalsmithing, ceramics, prints, installations, murals, and so on) as opposed to music, literature, drama, dance, and so on. When I use *a*Art, or sometimes *a*Arts, I refer to this collectivity -- visual art, music, literature, drama, dance and so on -- or the arts.

canonical or even chauvinistic capital and standard a. *a*Art is fluid, learning, growing, conversing, revising, expressing, considering. It is living and evolving. Our language must begin to recognize and acknowledge this.

*a*Art is processes and products.

The involvement of creating art gets the process and product treatment as well -- so, *p*Painting, *w*Writing, *c*Composing, *c*Choreographing, *f*Filmmaking, and so on.

We started *p*Painting in caves and so became modern humans. aArt is a human way of knowing. It is not merely a core way of knowing; it is not first among equals; *a*Art is the prerequisite way of human knowing.

Art is primitive brain stem. *a*Art is cerebral cortex.

Art criminally abides anemic curation and seven-second gawking. *a*Art employs thick curation and 7-spot engagement.

Art does not always have to be *a*Art but it does some of the time.

Artists and art enthusiasts do not always have to engage *a*Art but they do some of the time.

A fraction of the time if that's all they can muster.

This is why this flag illustration is so spot on. The empty square represents the amount of your art budget -- a sliver -- that needs to go to *a*Art and Wowsa Club (and so to the Prairie Filaments Cultural Substrate.) Of course, you could direct much more financially toward *a*Art.

The empty square also denotes how much engagement with art needs to be devoted to *a*Art. Again, a fraction; though you will eventually transition to *a*Art and leave art behind. For now, you don't have to involve yourself with *a*Art all the time or most of the time. But you do, if you want to claim to be an actualizing and authentic human, need to involve yourself with *a*Art some of the time.

*a*Art is learning template, emotional-cognitive lift, and sherpa for exploring meta-analytical ethnospheric understanding -- the floor <u>and</u> residence for actualizing and authentic humanity.

*a*Art is sage for lifelong learning. *a*Art is perspective and insight for community well-being. *a*Art is not luxurious, extraneous, or expendable. *a*Art is essential and core humanity.

Let's go back to our flag graphic. The solid squares can represent art. The lonely empty square can represent *a*Art. Let's take baby steps. You can live in art most of the time. You can believe that art is about technique and inquiries into light and shadow, foreground and background, materials and color. You can live in delusions that proclivitous beauty is beauty and that tame truths of monolithisms and dichotomies are truths. You can use art for escape, diversion, entertainment, commodification, trophy taking, social marking, and something to do. But, like the graphic above, if you want art to truly have its enlightening, healing, and inspirational powers, you will need to at least live a sliver of your time in *a*Art: emotional-cognitive lift; pluripotency actualized; meta-analytical ethnospheric understanding.

Meta

Many people spend almost no time in the meta level. Those who do often do not like it. The meta level, though, is where humanity actualizes, coalesces, and blossoms.

For our purpose, meta will mean the generative and undesignated state from which a dynamic and robust portfolio of specific and practiced substates can be known.

Many people, sadly, live in just one substate, something they claim is an identity -- and, more so, a claimed preordained, biological, and immutable identity -- of very anemic portfolio. Even more people, tragically, only live superficially and ignorant in that substate -- accepting all its culturally-constructed and imposed elements as their natural composition and taking face value explanations of themselves, others, and community as dogma.

Meta is the greeting: a signal of welcome, interaction, mutuality. The wink, the handshake, the bow, the curtsy, the fist bump, the nod, the "Hello," the hug, the smile -- these are all substates. One culture may predominantly use the nod; while another culture uses the handshake. But any and virtually all elements from this universe of substates can become part of anyone's portfolio. No one has to be so fractional, superficial, ignorant, or anemic in any dimension or facet of human life. Everyone, understanding the meta state, can have robust portfolios in every aspect of human expression and interaction.

Food is a basic contributor to one's familial, cultural, or ethnic identity. But, of course, food (and specific dishes) is a meta state, too. Your family celebrates birthdays with a dessert of strawberry rhubarb pie; another family celebrates with lemon meringue pie. Your ethnicity celebrates birthdays with milk cake; another ethnicity celebrates with pecan pie. The meta state is "desserts prepared for birthday celebrations." Think of all the desserts in the world. Why would you starve your portfolio to anemia to know just one or two desserts?

Meta is also connection, conversation, relationship, collaboration, and interaction: the filaments and connective tissue that energize and enrich everything human.

Art resides more in the anemic portfolio. An artist who only paints or who only paints flowers or who only paints lilies. A conductor who privileges composers born before 1900. A songwriter who only writes about burned out love. These are all "letters" that can be used in an "alphabet." but they are not the alphabet. And they are certainly not a language or narrative or cognizance emergent from the alphabet.

*a*Art orchestrates a robust portfolio -- but it's not even a portfolio of a multitude of art and artists. It's a portfolio of a multitude of conversations, connections, interactions, collaborations, and relationships among art, artists, art enthusiasts, and humanity. *a*Art is the relationship and conversation among paintings in an artist's exhibition or on a musician's album. *a*Art is the relationship and conversation among paintings in different exhibitions of the artist and on different albums of the musician. *a*Art is the relationship and conversation among the artist's paintings and others' paintings. *a*Art is the relationship among the musician's songs and others' songs. And on and on. I think you can get the idea.

In art, the substance is the painting, the song, the poem, the play, the dance, the story. In *a*Art the substance is the painting's conversation with the world, the song's interaction with humanity, the poem's relationship with community, the play's collaboration with human discourse, the dance's connection with meaning and understanding, and the story's engagement with the human cultural and knowledge treasures.* *a*Art is meta, and meta is conversation, interaction, relationship, collaboration, connection, and engagement.

*In this sentence, all participants can be interchanged. "... the painting's conversation with the world ..." can become "... the painting's connection with the world ..." or "... the painting's conversation with human discourse ..." Or it can become "... the painting's conversation with the world, humanity, community, human discourse, meaning and understanding, and human cultural and knowledge treasure ..." Or it can become "... the painting's conversation, relationship, collaboration, connection, and engagement with the world ..." Or, as you've discerened by not, the sentence can become any combination of the painting, song, poem, play, dance, and story's conversation, interaction, relationship, collaboration, connection, and engagement with the world, humanity, community, human discourse, meaning and understanding, and human cultural and knowledge treasures.

Meta-analytical ethnospheric understanding (maeu)

Meta-analytical ethnospheric understanding (maeu) is the highest form of emotional-cognitive development. It is the site of human actualization and the evolution/transcendence to a new human species (from *Homo sapiens sapiens* to *Homo adrians robustes.* *) maeu is Level 7 (mKG7) on the muller Kohlberg Gilligan Revised Scale of Emotional-Cognitive Development.

Meta-analysis, here, is applying the meta state to one's portfolio and infusing it with robustness. (Please last vignette, "Meta.") Ethnosphere was conceptualized by photographer Wade Davis. I have updated his definition: the ethnosphere is the dynamic sum total of all the world's peoples, cultures, histories, traditions, ideas, narratives, and artifacts. maeu means curating a robust portfolio across all one's human dimensions and aspects.

maeu is a toolbox or palette from which to constantly author and re-author oneself robustly and authentically.

Every day, a human being responds to tasks and impulses. When one responds to a task or impulse with a face value response given by society, one becomes an impostor human. When one responds with one or two options, one becomes an anemic human, usually the existence of *Homo sapiens sapiens* -- the vicious defender of identity. When one responds with a dynamic and robust portfolio of options, one becomes an authentic human, the nascent and emergent and authentic existence of *Homo adrians robustes* -- the advocate of supra-identity or ethnospheric identity.

*a*Art is the annotating, articulation, energizing, illuminating, and invigorating tapestry for meta-analytical ethnospheric understanding.

*Homo adrians robustes originally was termed *Homo adrians paradoxes*. This nomenclature changed midway through year 60 in the Adrianic calendar on June 23. (June 23, 2021 Common Era or June 23, 60 Anno Robustes.) Anno Paradoxes was also changed to Anno Robustes on this date. (A.P. to A.R.) The Adrianic Calendar commenced on January 17, 1961 and started the year 0 A.P. (now 0 A.R.) The term paradox (which could accommodate chaos and order, light and dark, reason and emotion) still wasn't has sophisticated and accommodating as robustness; just as equilibrium is not as sophisticated as homeostasis in chemistry and biology. Humanity needs a term capable of housing dynamism and multifacetedness. Robustness can do that more than paradox can.

Human

When we started *p*Painting in caves, we became human. *a*Art is the prerequisite way of human knowing and was the capacity for human emergence.

Some will say we became human via toolmaking, language, agriculture, or cooking. But those are all abstractions. *a*Art is the pure or wellspring abstraction.

The vertebrae, muscles, nervous system, and circulatory system of the *a*Arts are abstractions, metaphors, ideas, imaginations, stories, framings, visions, models, symbols, representations -- they are the human tools. The tools of *a*Art are the tools of humanity.

Humans are:
- abstraction farmers
- metaphor wranglers
- symbol conductors
- storytellers

Humans adapt nature's original purpose. The emergence of tools fits this statement exactly. The branch became a backscratcher. The animal's pelt became a piece of warm clothing. The rock became a hunting projectile. Woven plant fiber became a roof protecting from the rain.

Humans, as much as they can, do not let biology indelibly shape them. The developed myopia is corrected with lenses. *We don't accept biology and we embrace cultural construction.* The potentially fatal infection is terminated with antibiotics. *We don't accept biology and we embrace cultural construction.* The life-ending automobile accident with multiple internal injuries and broken bones and massive blood loss is repaired in the trauma center. *We don't accept biology and we embrace cultural construction.*

We don't accept biology and we embrace cultural construction.

(And we should and must apply this mantra to human identities, interactions, and relationships.)

For humans, truth is sentient and empathic interpretation of facts.

For humans, nature is culture.

For humans, the literal is figurative.

For humans, reality is constructed.

Humans are not ensconced in identities and ideologies because identities and ideologies cannot accommodate their pluripotency manifested through meta-analytical ethnospheric understanding.

Humans' greatest roles are citizen, neighbor, life coach, friend, creative, critical thinker, conversationalist, caregiver, learner, collaborator, and meaning maker.

Humans' greatest legacy is the life of consideration, creative engagement, critical thinking, and connections they leave behind.

Idle Capacity and Day Dreams

I've always appreciated William Calvin's conjecture on the formation of our big brains. It takes incredible neuronal connections to throw a projectile (a stone, then a spear) across a great distance and strike a moving, fleeing target with such lethal accuracy to make a kill for dinner. As these neuronal connections developed, grew, and evolve, they may our forebears fine hunters.

But hunting is a very sporadic activity. Most of the time the neurons and the neural pathways that allowed fine eye-hand-muscle coordination sat around idle. And they began talking to one another.

This talk became human consciousness.

This frivolity -- talk doesn't kill the beast for dinner -- this adaptation, created imagination; and imagination started *d*Drawing on walls* at Chauvet, Lascaux,

Atepuerca, Sulawesi, El Castillo, La Ferrassie, Blombos, Bhimbetka, and Daraki-Chattan.

We started *p*Painting in caves and so became human.

      * Not all early art is in caves. There is art on rocks and egg shells as well as small sculptures. And not all the early art is by Homo sapiens. El Castillo and La Ferrassie may be by Homo neanderthalensis. The "Venus of Berekhat Ram" (if it holds as human art) and the Bhimbetka and Daraki-Chattan Cupules would have to have been made by Homo erectus or other earlier homonids.

      Also, "we started *p*Painting in caves and then became human" is not a magical, immediate thing. We see this process happened across species and across millennia. It is a powerful way to think of ourselves as creative beings.

      And, of course, many other processes and developments made us human -- but this metaphor of creative capacity still nails it -- giving meaning to our imaginative and expressive essence and anchoring *a*Art as integral and essential to being richly and authentically human.

The Second Wowsa Club Badge
I will live a creative life

Every human being, every day, authors, performs, and curates life. Every human being seeks understanding and makes meaning from experiences, learning, knowledge, and informed sources. Every human being spends the day interpreting and understanding.

Above and beyond this, a human being could and is welcome to become a painter, writer, composer, musician, playwright, actor, choreographer, film director, cinematographer, or dancer. But that is not the creative life of which we speak. It is the creative life of authoring, performing, and curating that is every human's obligation and opportunity.

The creative human being knows the power of storytelling and visioning and meaning making the *a*Arts provide for the enrichment, fortification, and reinvigoration of one's life. The creative human being does enthusiastically and knowledgeably engage the formal aArtisic community because the creative human is aware of the resources and riches and essentialities the formal or professional grade storytellers and meaning makers contribute to human existence.

The Third Wowsa Club Badge
I am an Everyone Creative Champion

*a*Art truly begins when a work-of-art enters conversation, relationship, collaboration, interaction, connection, and consideration with other art, artists, art enthusiasts, community, milieu, ethnosphere, and humanity. These filaments, connective tissues and circulatory/musculature/skeletal/nervous systems are the substance of *a*Art.

(Individual works-of-art are comparable to amino acids and carbohydrates -- building blocks, letters in an alphabet.)

The Everyone Creative Champion infuses the creative human enterprise with energy and life -- involving and engaging *a*Artistic activity; making *a*Arts central to one's daily life; and contributing to a substantive and ubiquitous conversation in daily life about the *a*Arts.

The Everyone Creative Champion modestly, specifically, and pragmatically contributes to the nourishment of the artsphere (arts ecosphere) through the support of the Prairie Filaments Cultural Substrate.

The Fourth Wowsa Club Badge
The aArts
are
the prerequisite
way of human knowing

We started *p*Painting in caves and then became human. Expanding upon Phillip Phenix, there are many ways of human knowing: anthropology, *a*Arts, economics, education, history, languages and linguistics, law, mathematics, medicine and healing disciplines, philosophy, physical education, political science, psychology, rhetoric, science, sociology, and ultimate concern. The *a*Arts are more than first among equals of these ways of knowing. The *a*Arts are the prerequisite way of human knowing.

*a*Art, then Human.

The Fifth Wowsa Club Badge
aArt, Then Human

It cannot be said enough. Humans started pPainting in caves and so became human. *a*Art, then human.

Imagining, Creating (Storytelling, Visioning, Inquiring, Framing, Interpreting, Meaning Making), Conversing, Connecting. Learning. Teaching. These are the human activities, and they emanate from our *a*Artistic capacities for abstraction, adaptation, and culturally constructing.

The Sixth Wowsa Club Badge
I am a Participart

Wowsa Club badge earners help underwrite the Prairie Filaments Cultural Substrate which nourishes the artsphere, vibrant communities enriched by the *a*Arts, and the United *a*Arts of America.

*a*Art has progressed to emotional-cognitive lift and articulation of meta-analytical ethnospheric understanding.

*a*Artists are purveyors of emotional-cognitive lift, perspective, insight, storytelling, visioning, meaning making, and understanding.

Audiences, spectators, and gawkers are extinct or entirely irrelevant. They are replaced by informed and engaged arts enthusiasts called participarts (participants in art.) Participarts are integral agents in communities vibrant with enriching arts activity.

Participarts are never passive spectators. They engage in prework, cowork, postwork, and *a*Arts advocacy just by being enthusiast and earnest collaborators with *a*Arts. Participarts are *a*Arts champions.

The Seventh Wowsa Club Badge
The aArts as Community Thought Leader

The aArts are an accessible, affordable, and almost inexhaustible wellspring of stories, visions, framings, interpretations, narratives, conversations, perspectives, insights, lessons, explorations, inquiries, meaning makings, options, pathways, and possibilities for individuals and communities. The aArts are community thought leaders.

Community leaders will do well to involve artists in conversations of community building, problem resolution, opportunity taking, visioning, planning, implementing, evaluating, and revising.

The Eighth Wowsa Club Badge
The aArts are essential to daily life

The *a*Arts are as essential to daily life as good nutrition, exercise, self-care, exploring, learning, conversation, and connection.

That statement is so powerful, I need to add nothing to it.

Parsings (Definitions) and Details

Parsings

A ***modest proposal of immense proportions***, powered by you -- creative champion and profound storyteller -- powered by us, to nourish engaged and aware community, informed and civil dialogue, vibrant **aArtsphere** (*a*Arts ecosphere) personal enrichment and exuberance, and human actualization by igniting and sustaining a **cultural substrate** (specifically the **Prairie Filaments Cultural Substrate**) with eventually 728 invigoration modes, fueled by participarts in the Wowsa Club and fortified by satellite **Red Door Neighborhood Catalysts and Cosmic Third Places** to author conversational, collaborative, resilient, empathic, optimistic, adaptive, sentient, welcoming, curious, explorative, anchoring, critically thinking, and meaning making interactions in a complementary **United *a*Arts of America.**

aArtsphere -- an ecosystem or ecosphere of the aArts composed of aArts, aArtists, participarts, curators, cultural presenters, aArt historians, and communities supportive of aArtistic activity.

Cultural substrate -- infrastructure for the aArts that includes attitudes, facilities, programming, community engagement, and activities deeply, broadly, resiliiently, invigoratingly, and consistently supportive of the aArts.

Prairie Filaments Cultural Substrate -- the specific and inaugural formal cultural substrate that can take the aArts to new levels and cement their place as essential, integral elements of neighborhoods, communities, organizations, and individual lives.

The aspiration is for it to one day have 728, or more, invigoration nodes: mechanisms of major and enduring financial and attitudinal support which will fortify and enliven the overall tenor for the aArts in the community and region.

Red Door Neighborhood Catalyst and Cosmic Third Place (aka Red Door) -- Red Door will be many things -- gathering place, ideas and innovation studio, aArt gallery and performance space, retail incubator, community builder, conversation starter, healing house, cultural center.

Red Door headquarters will be a place of exploration and capital for United aArts of America as well as headquarters for the Wowsa Club. It will have a Consideration Cafe and be home to red dor -- a 6,000-square-foot interactive, sentient, living, and evolving destination pPainting.

Red Door will also be satellited or franchised. And so like quaint Carnegie libraries, there will be small versions of Red Door all over the country serving as hospitable sites for creatives, dreamers, doers, collaborators and connectors. Most of them, hopefully, will have a Consideration Cafe.

United *a*Arts of America -- All this activity aspires to engender a citizenry, a humanity: informed, aware, engaged, involved, empathic, sentient, explorative, learning, imaginative, expressive, conversant, connected, at home in abstraction, fluent in metaphor, comprehending of cultural construction, consciously adaptative, ecstatic in dynamic multifariousness, and exuberant.

The Ninth Wowsa Club Badge
I am exuberant

I will use meta-analytical ethnospheric understanding and employ the ethnosphere as my palette to harness my pluripotency and become dynamic, multifarious, and exuberant.

The Tenth Wowsa Club Badge
I am
a self-authored and community-colored
performance

Each day we write ourselves, paint ourselves, compose ourselves, choreograph ourselves, sing ourselves, dance ourselves, act ourselves, and perform ourselves. Why not be a magical performance of fluidity and multifariousness? After all, fluidity is our stability and multifariousness is our singularity.

Details

    Badges are nominally priced, not tax-deductible, and certified/blessed by four artists you help support.

    Again, please look at our flag graphic above. In 2021 dollars, most badges will be priced between nine and seventeen dollars, with the nine badges featured in this book priced at nine dollars. Nourishing the Prairie Filaments Cultural Substrate and sustaining a vibrant *a*Artsphere is not meant to be expensive or a drain on one's *a*Arts budget. Wowsa Club is a type of massive crowdsourcing. Nominal, modest contributions can result in outcomes of immense, sea change proportions.

    The black squares of the flag represent all your established and extant financial expenditures on the arts.

The empty black square represents a new sliver of support for the Prairie Filaments Cultural Substrate.

Wowsa Club hopes to attract tens of millions to *a*Arts engagement who have not been that involved in the *a*Arts. For them, in the flag, the black squares represent all their interests, passions, activities, and priorities. The empty square represents their first sliver of foray into the arts via Wowsa Club and the Prairie Filaments Cultural Substrate.

*a*Arts Champions will earn badges and those badges will eventually be certified/blessed by four artists. Those four artists will receive a small compensation. When you earn a badge, you will not only support the aArtsphere, you will support four living artists.

The price of a badge is not tax-deductible. Wowsa Club, Red Door, and Consideration Cafe will operate as for-profit concerns. Red Door wants to contribute to a world where the *a*Arts can make it on their own, where the *a*Artsphere is supportive and vibrant and creativity has essential and integral daily engagement. The *a*Arts can thrive because people earnestly engage them and *a*Arts are not seen as superfluous, trivial, extraneous, luxurious, unnecessary, or expendable.

Loose Strategies

Everything is open to revision and refinement.

*a*Arts Champions and Wowsa Club

aArts Champions will earn badges and express their earnest support for the arts. The revenues from the badges will be accumulated in the Wowsa Club.

Wowsa Club A: Red Door

Wowsa Club revenues will underwrite Red Door Neighborhood Catalyst and Cosmic Third Place.

Initial Wowsa Club revenues will be funneled to these priorities:

1. modest salary for director and modest fund for operations;
2. deferred maintenance on, innovations for, and purchase of I'm Sorry Palace -- the house where the *a*Artsphere, cultural substrate, Prairie Filaments Cultural Substrate; Red Door, Wowsa Club, the badges, *a*Art, the *a*Art genome, Consideration Cafe, the participart, and United aArts of America were conceived;
3. the inaugural Red Door with headquarters, *red dor* destination *p*Painting, and Consideration Cafe;
4. the first couple satellite Red Door franchises; and

5. endowments for the director's position and for an operating fund.

Wowsa Club B: Prairie Filaments

Wowsa Club revenues will underwrite the Prairie Filaments Cultural Substrate that will eventually support 728 innovation nodes across fifty states, the District of Columbia, and Puerto Rico. Innovation nodes will be mechanisms of enduring financial support for selected cultural organizations or initiatives or for artists. (Some of these nodes may rotate among new recipients.) The nodes will not provide support all aArtists and organizations, but they will stimulate a tenor of enthusiasm for and involvement in the arts community.

The plan, initially, will be to get four depthful nodes in a state, one in each "quadrant," to inaugurate a breadth of momentum. Then the substrate will have depth and breadth. Then the hope will be to get fourteen nodes per state. And then to add even more -- four to eight that could definitely be rotated among new recipients.

Wowsa Club C: Activated Filaments

Wowsa Club revenues will eventually provide a wonderful meta or supra state to Red Door and Prairie Filaments' activities by underwriting innovation filaments of conversation and connections among activities of the innovation nodes, their host *a*Artistic and regular communities, and participarts all over.

United *a*Arts of America

All this Wowsa Club activity and Red Door presence/shepherding/mentoring will create a nation where citizens take learning, critical thinking, imagination, and creativity seriously and where the *a*Arts are recognized and practiced as essential and integral daily elements of human existence that add resourceful andinvaluable inputs to meaning making, understanding, and the actualization of authentic human life.

Introduction and Activation

Introduction

Patrick Muller is an *a*Arts advocate and strategist, *a*Artist, healer, scholar, and teacher. As a *p*Painter, Muller works under the name Hanpo. Muller is also a participart, attending many *a*Arts events, and avidly collecting the works of over 300 living *a*Artists.

The conceptualizations of Red Door Neighborhood Catalyst and Cosmic Third Place and the Prairie Filaments Cultural Substrate, in some forms, have been decades in the making. The conceptualizations of aArts champions and Wowsa Club -- the mechanism that can make Red Door and Prairie Filaments happen -- are of more recent vintage.

That is enough biography for now. Red Door and Prairie Filaments need to be sketched, chronicled, and realized. Then, Muller says, his biography will be worth noting.

Activation

Please join the Wowsa Club and become an *a*Arts champion today by visiting:

wowsa.club

Invitation

Four more badges

The Eleventh Wowsa Club Badge
Find Us Home

Most of the work Prairie Filaments Cultural Substrate will do will be "invisible." Collaborating, connecting, supporting. The outcome of Prairie Filaments' work will be to strengthen cultural organizations and the work of aArtists and to help them with their programming and creativity. But those outcomes will be behind the scenes.

Prairie Filaments, for the most part, will not collect, exhibit, perform, or present aArt. It will make the collecting, exhibiting, performing, and presenting of aArt better.

The inaugural Red Door Neighborhood Catalyst and Cosmic Third Place, which will be the headquarters of

Prairie Filaments' activities, will be visible and tangible. It will be a place participarts and others can visit and engage.

It is crucial to have this tangible, palpable site of interaction to nourish the cultural substrate and engender the United aArts of America.

Participarts who earn this badge will accelerate the building of the first Red Door; and that is an oh-so-important first step to get this *a*Arts movement going.

The Twelfth (and Repeatable) Wowsa Club Badge
Artober Caucus

It would have been similar for Republicans if they didn't have an incumbent president, but for Democrats in 2020, they were around 30 well-known candidates initially vying for the Democratic nomination. In order to make participant numbers for debates manageable, some thinning out had to occur. Candidates had to meet parameters (in polling and/or number of financial supporters across a certain number of states) in order to be eligible for debates.

So candidates started asking potential supporters for contributions as small as a dollar just to get new supporters on the rolls. And candidates started raising millions of dollars in just a matter of days or a weekend. The Artober

Caucus applies this strategy to raising funds for the Prairie Filaments Cultural Substrate.

Without political ideology and with only the love for the *a*Arts, the Artober Caucus badge can attract millions of "caucus goers" (contributors) and several innovations nodes can be underwritten over the course of a weekend.

Artober Caucus will be repeated periodically, which is why it's a repeatable badge.

The Thirteenth Wowsa Club Badge
The Zero Amendment

The First Amendment to the United States Constitution guarantees free speech, which has evolved now to free expression. But even before expression is imagination which germinates abstraction, creativity, and ideas. So we have created The Zero Amendment for the right to imagination and the essentiality to create. The badge will allow participarts and *a*Arts champions to become signatories on the amendment.

The amendment will be housed at the Inaugural Red Door Neighborhood Catalyst and Cosmic Third Place.

The Fourteenth (and Repeatable) Wowsa Club Badge
Adrian's Day

Every June 23rd will be celebrated as Adrian's International Day for Arts and Humanities, or Adrian's Day. The festival day will celebrate the arts and humanities and raise funds for them, especially to nourish the vessel of the Prairie Filaments Cultural Substrate. As Adrian's Day will be an annual event, this badge is repeatable.

Thank Yous

Thank You A

Thank you for reading.

Thank You B

Thank you especially for participating in the
Wowsa Club and earning some of its badges.

Thank You C

Thank you for inking your name on human creativity. In so doing, you are becoming an advocate for and practitioner of *a*Arts as essential and integral to daily life and human actualization. You are comfortable with abstraction, metaphor, and cultural construction. You are aware, informed, engaged, and conversational. You are a storyteller, writing and performing your newly each day. And you are aware of the rich resources the aArts add to the community in insight, perspective, options, possibilities, meaning making, empathy, critical thinking and understanding. You are an *a*Arts champion.